THE TREE AND YOUR MINISTRY

Dag Heward-Mills

Parchment House

THE TREE AND YOUR MINISTRY

Copyright © 2008 Dag Heward-Mills

First Published 2008 by Lux Verbi BM
(Pty) Ltd, P O Box 5, Wellington 7654,
South Africa Reg no 1953/000037/07
ISBN 13: 978-0-7963-0864-1

First published 2008 by Parchment House
5th Printing 2020

Find out more about Dag Heward-Mills at:

Healing Jesus Campaign
Email: evangelist@daghewardmills.org
Website: www.daghewardmills.org
Facebook: Dag Heward-Mills
Twitter: @EvangelistDag

ISBN : 978-1-68398-248-7

Contents

Contents

CHAPTER 1

The Tree of the Knowledge of Good and Evil

And out of the ground made the LORD God to grow every tree that is pleasant to the sight, and good for food; the tree of life also in the midst of the garden, and THE TREE OF KNOWLEDGE OF GOOD AND EVIL.

Genesis 2:9

Most Christians do not understand the place of the tree of the knowledge of good and evil in our lives. We often think it is an ancient tree which existed in the time of Adam and Eve. We believe that this tree had poisonous fruit which once eaten, would kill the eater.

Unfortunately, Adam and Eve ate of this tree and died. When we read this story, we think to ourselves, "It was a pity for Adam and Eve to have eaten this poisonous fruit and thankfully we will never be tempted by such a tree".

Alas, we will have to deal with this same tree and its fruits. What you must realize is that the tree of the knowledge of good and evil is still in existence today. It presents the same temptation to us as it did to Adam and Eve. *It presents itself as an alternative to God.*

Once you have eaten of this tree, you know what is right and what is wrong. You know things that are good and things that are evil. Once you are armed with this knowledge (of what is right and what is wrong) you don't really need God to tell you what to do. You can navigate through life and ministry using the knowledge you have acquired.

It is not apparent to the shallow thinker what devastating effects the knowledge of good and evil can have. After all, it is not the knowledge of evil, but the knowledge of good and evil. This tree does one thing to you and it is the worst thing possible! It separates you from the guidance of God and dependence on Him.

As you grow in experience in this life, you gradually assimilate the knowledge of good and evil. By the time you are seventeen years old, you probably know of many things that are good for you or are evil for you. This is the knowledge that comes to all mankind. Now comes the difference between Christians and non-Christians.

Non-Christians and the Tree

Non-Christians continue to live, doing things that are evil whilst justifying themselves continually. They especially justify their lives by referring to the good things that they do as being the basis for being okay.

Since they know what is good and what is evil, they do not need to go to church, to pray or to serve God. This creates a large group of people who live without God simply because they think they know what is right and wrong in this life.

Once they do a few good things, they justify themselves and overlook any evil they may be involved in.

Another group of people who have eaten of this tree think that religion is unnecessary, and that many church activities are simply a waste of time. The reading of the Bible is frivolous and a waste of time; once some moral standards are kept, everyone will be okay.

Such people even think that the priest is trying to maintain his job by creating unnecessary little by-laws to keep the congregation under control.

Unfortunately, this is where the perversions of mankind make their entry. In Europe, homosexuality is considered as good and not evil, whereas having sex with little children is considered to be evil and not good.

This self-determined standard of good and evil has thereby created a perverted world of twisted human beings living without God.

Europe has people who are perfect examples of those who have eaten of the tree of good and evil and excluded God completely from their lives. Europeans chase murderers around the world and prosecute people who commit war crimes and genocide with a passion.

They believe in what they understand to be right. Meanwhile, they destroy the fabric of their society by allowing men to marry men and teaching homosexuality to children in schools.

Very few Europeans would ever go to church. Their cathedrals and church buildings are empty on Sunday mornings. On Sunday morning, European families enjoy breakfast and have a good family time together since they consider that to be a good thing. Church is now frivolous and unnecessary to them.

You can see how subtly but powerfully the knowledge of good and evil has eliminated God from our lives and created a lost and desolate race of human beings.

Christians and the Tree

Desolation comes into the life of Christians through this same tree. After serving God for a while, Christians know more about the laws of God and assume that they know what is right and what is wrong.

This way of thinking is what creates a separation between God and so-called mature Christians. It seems that people who have been Christians for some time are in the greatest danger from this tree. Long-standing Christians exclude God from their lives by holding onto what they know to be right or wrong and not being open to what God may be currently doing.

Have you wondered why God does new things and starts new movements through outsiders and young people? The older, established Christians and institutions often know too much to be open to God. *God is often excluded from the minds and hearts of those who have served Him for a long time.* This is a frightening but real phenomenon.

I am writing about this because Christians must recognize its reality before they are poisoned by their knowledge of good and evil.

CHAPTER 2

Jesus and the Tree Eaters

And out of the ground made the LORD God to grow every tree that is pleasant to the sight, and good for food; the tree of life also in the midst of the garden, and THE TREE OF KNOWLEDGE OF GOOD AND EVIL.

Genesis 2:9

The people who fought against Jesus Christ were not irreligious sinners. The people who crucified our Saviour were the most established religious leaders of the day.

They knew what was right and what was wrong. They fasted, they prayed, they paid tithes, and did all that was right in their eyes to the exclusion of God and His Son Jesus Christ.

On the night that Jesus was betrayed and crucified, prostitutes, drunkards and murderers were asleep in bed and did not rise up to harm our Saviour.

The "good" people who knew all about God and whose profession it was to write the Scriptures (the Scribes) were at the forefront of the mob that could not recognize the Messiah.

The pastors of the day, the highest Priests, invented charges and accused the holiest and the best. They made Him out to be the worst of scum and declared Him unfit to live.

This reality should send chills down the spines of long-standing Christians or religious persons who claim to be in the service of God.

Please learn this truth: Serving God for a long time puts you at risk of depending on the tree of good and evil rather than depending on God.

The tree of good and evil actually blinds you and prevents you from seeing God. This is why Jesus said that sinners and publicans will enter the kingdom faster than Pharisees and religious leaders would. They were too religious and knew too much.

...Jesus saith unto them, Verily I say unto you, That the publicans and the harlots go into the kingdom of God before you.

Matthew 21:31

The lesson is simply this: We must not depend on what we know. We must depend on God. We must love God and know God. We must follow God and get close to Him.

God cannot be substituted for a set of rules or principles. God is not a book. He is much more than a book. Loving God and focusing on God is a hundred times greater than knowing many things about God and religion.

That is what Paul meant when he said the love of Christ surpasses knowledge.

And to know the LOVE OF CHRIST, which PASSETH KNOWLEDGE, that ye might be filled with all the fulness of God.

Ephesians 3:19

The Tree and the Church

It is this same tree that turns ministries into centres of desolation and rivers of death. Churches that once breathed life into the whole world often become the enemies of God. Observe carefully how churches that once ministered life to thousands, become institutionalized centres of opposition to the move of God. The power and the life of God that led to the Reformation can hardly be found in these reformed churches.

John Wesley, the founder of the Methodist church, is one of my favourite people. I visited his home in London and toured the church that he built. I was shown the different rooms of John Wesley's house. I then toured the church that he built and visited the museum that stands to his memory. Finally, we stood in the little cemetery behind the church where John Wesley is buried and read his epitaph.

It was an interesting tour but the final comment by my tour guide saddened me and set me thinking.

He said, "Unfortunately, the Methodist church today is much in the same state in which John Wesley found the Church of England."

The revival which he brought to the Church of England and which gave rise to Methodism is much needed in the Methodist church today.

I thought of myself and the church which I have pastured and nurtured. I wondered what would become of this ministry in some years to come.

The Tree and the Minister

When God calls you to ministry, you have a passion to follow Him and to do whatever He says. After a season of obeying God, you discover for yourself how true the Word of God is.

You discover how prayer works. You discover the importance of the Bible and the truths of the Bible.

After a few years of serving God, it seems that you know everything and there is a silent but deadly assumption that you have found the keys to life and ministry.

It is easy to stop seeking God and to rely on the knowledge that you have acquired. You may be filled with the knowledge acquired from your experiences and years of serving the Lord.

Amazingly, it is this knowledge of good and evil that brings about an overwhelming desolation in the life of a minister.

Staying Fresh

I have found myself having to seek God all the time in order to stay fresh. Seeking God does not just mean having extended times of prayers. It also means fighting to know the mind of God for your life today.

It means not depending on what you know already but being open to know any fresh revelation and guidance from the Lord.

That is what will ensure the intensity, vividness, clarity and newness in the spirit of every minister.

Unfortunately, the intensity of the ministry diminishes as preachers depend more and more on the knowledge of good and evil that they have acquired over the years. They lose their sharpness, their vividness and their cutting-edge appeal.

After a while, many can see the dullness, the dreariness and the lifelessness of the pastor and his ministry.

I Watched It Happen

I have not been in the ministry for so long, but even in the few years of my ministry, I have seen people who started out very powerfully but after a while could not keep up with what God was doing.

Some pastors, who were involved in the work of ministry at the early stages of our church, simply could not transition when God was doing a new thing.

Somehow, they fell behind and became offended by new things and by the appearance of new people in the ministry.

My best people are always my oldest people. The longer I have known someone, the more relaxed I become with the person. I would always prefer to work with those who have stayed around longest but unfortunately that was not to be the case. As I moved on to different phases of the ministry, some of the older people felt the good old ways were the best ways.

Dear pastor, the good old ways are not always the best ways. Perhaps, you feel that way because you are stuck in your ways. And being full of the knowledge of what is right and what is wrong, you are unable to transition and rise to the next level of your calling.

There are many things that I did in the early part of my ministry which were good and biblical.

Surprisingly, God does not want me to do some of these good and biblical things anymore. The fact is, these good and biblical things do not work anymore today as they did yesterday.

Your church may have been independent for years, but becoming part of a denomination may be God's will for you today.

Perhaps independence worked for some years, but will not work anymore from henceforth.

Perhaps being a lay person worked very well for years, but now it is important to be full-time in the ministry.

Perhaps insisting on your rights may have brought you far in your marriage and in your life, but now yielding and obeying may be the key.

Parting with God

It is at this point that most pastors part with God. *God continues in one direction and we go on in another direction based on our knowledge of what is right and what is wrong.*

Parting with God is silent but deadly, like cancer. Samson did not know that he had parted with the Holy Spirit.

And she said, The Philistines be upon thee, Samson. And he awoke out of his sleep, and said, I will go out as at other times before, and shake myself. AND HE WIST NOT THAT THE LORD WAS DEPARTED FROM HIM.

Judges 16:20

In many cases, good pastors part with God when they have to choose between doing something they have traditionally known to be evil or good.

In order to follow God, you will have to do things that everyone considers to be "not good". At other times you will have to do things that are traditionally evil in order to follow God. At this point, God tests whether you owe your allegiance to Jehovah or to a set of rules and principles.

It is not easy for a good person to forsake what he knows to be good in order to do something else which is known to be evil or not proven to be good.

This is probably the greatest test of all ministry. Will you continue to follow God in the truest sense of the word or will you follow rules and ideologies just because they are good and proven.

CHAPTER 3

The Crossroads of Ministry

And out of the ground made the LORD God to grow every tree that is pleasant to the sight, and good for food; the tree of life also in the midst of the garden, and THE TREE OF KNOWLEDGE OF GOOD AND EVIL.

Genesis 2:9

The Ultimate test of Ministry

I want to show you several men of God who faced this ultimate test of ministry. It is at this point that they revealed who they were serving: God or a book.

1.   Abraham at the Crossroads

And he said, TAKE NOW THY SON, thine only son Isaac, whom thou lovest, and get thee into the land of Moriah; AND OFFER HIM THERE FOR A BURNT OFFERING ...

Genesis 22:2

Abraham reached this crossroads when the Lord told him to do what was traditionally evil. The Lord asked him to murder his son. The tree of the knowledge of good and evil would most assuredly tell you that it is a bad thing to kill your son! Traditionally, it is an evil thing to kill but it was in obeying this command that Abraham stayed close to God and became special to God. God decided to bless Abraham specially.

And said, By myself have I sworn, saith the LORD, for BECAUSE THOU HAST DONE THIS thing, and hast not withheld thy son, thine only son: That in blessing I WILL BLESS THEE, and in multiplying I will multiply thy seed as the stars of the heaven, and as the sand which is upon the sea shore; and thy seed shall possess the gate of his enemies;

Genesis 22:16-17

Why did God decide to bless Abraham? Was it because Abraham had agreed to commit murder? It was because Abraham was more committed to God than to anything that he knew.

Do you want to stay close to God? Do you want to stay special to God? Then do not depend on what you know to be proven but trust God and follow Him. What I am sharing with you is deep and is for people who want to follow God at the highest level.

2. Joshua at the Crossroads

And they utterly destroyed all that was in the city, both MAN AND WOMAN, YOUNG AND OLD, and ox, and sheep, and ass, with the edge of the sword.

Joshua 6:21

Can I ask you a question? Is it right to kill someone? Is it right to kill innocent women and children? The answer is, "No." The tree of good and evil tells us so.

However, God said to Joshua, "Kill everyone: kill all the men, kill all the women, and kill all the children." That was God's will and decision for Joshua.

Joshua could either do what he thought was good or choose to obey God. Our demise begins when we part with God. Oh, what can you do without God? You may have your little book of rules but it has not the power to save, heal or deliver you.

3. Saul at the Crossroads

Is it good to make sacrifices to the Lord? The answer is, "YES". But God was angry with Saul because he made a sacrifice when he shouldn't have. Knowing the good thing and not doing it can be even harder for a seasoned minister of God. God did not want Saul to make sacrifices even though he enjoyed the sacrifices of His people. God called Saul's offering an act of foolishness.

Therefore said I, The Philistines will come down now upon me to Gilgal, and I have not made supplication unto the LORD: I forced myself therefore, and OFFERED A BURNT OFFERING. And Samuel said to Saul, THOU HAST DONE FOOLISHLY: thou hast not kept the commandment of the LORD thy God, which he commanded thee: for now would the LORD have established thy kingdom upon Israel for ever.

1 Samuel 13:12, 13

There are times God does not want me to pray for some people. Being a minister, it is difficult not to pray for someone. At certain levels, you can get yourself into trouble by praying for people and showing mercy when God is not showing mercy. I have found myself praying for people and God abandoning me whilst I was praying.

I asked the Lord, "Where are you, where is your power?" And He said to me, "Who asked you to do what you are doing?"

One day, the Lord told me not to accept one of my pastors if he came back to change his mind about certain decisions he had taken. The Lord was showing me that He knew more about the person than I did.

I had to obey God and reject the person when he came back. It was not easy for me, but I am not following a tree. I am following a living God. A few weeks later, I discovered things I didn't know about this fellow and I realized that just as the Lord said, I was dealing with more than I knew about.

4. David at the Crossroads

To know what is good and to withhold your hand from doing good can be one of the most difficult things for someone who has walked with God. But doing good can actually get you into trouble with God. King David wanted to build a temple. Is it not a good thing to build a temple? Is church planting and church building not our foremost quest?

Yet, God wanted David to refrain from building a church. After you have served God for years will He be able to tell you what to do and what not to do? Will you not be too experienced and knowledgeable to receive such absurd and non-biblical guidance? Would you not know what is good and right and just stick to it? This is where David would have parted with God.

But even in doing this good work, he consulted God because he knew that not all good things are God's will.

That the king said unto Nathan the prophet, See now, I dwell in an house of cedar, but the ark of God dwelleth within curtains.

2 Samuel 7:2

The point I am making is that we need to stay close to God. We need to be like David who constantly inquired of the Lord. He never assumed that he knew what was right or wrong.

After eating of the tree of the knowledge of good and evil, we begin to assume that we always know what is right or wrong. Remember, the longer you have served God, the more prone you are to this sin of desolation: substituting God for a tree of knowledge.

5. Hosea and the Tree

If I was looking for a wife today, how many of my friends and colleagues would approve of me marrying one of the prostitutes in my city. People would say I have gone mad. How many Christians would advise a young man who is zealous for the Lord to marry a prostitute? This is obviously something bad. In other words, it is not a good thing to do. The tree of good and evil would advise against any such nonsense!

However, that is exactly what God asked the prophet Hosea to do! In fact, that was the first thing that the Lord asked the prophet Hosea to do. He was to start his ministry by marrying one of the city's prostitutes.

The beginning of the word of the LORD by Hosea. And the LORD said to Hosea, Go, TAKE UNTO THEE A WIFE OF WHOREDOMS and children of whoredoms: for the land hath committed great whoredom, departing from the LORD.

Hosea 1:2

I am not writing this book so that you will go and do crazy things like committing murder and marrying strange women. I am writing this so that you will see that it is God Himself who rules in the lives of His true servants. To remain fresh and anointed, you need to be guided constantly by God and not by experience or by your traditions and ideals.

CHAPTER 4

The Apostles and the Tree

And out of the ground made the LORD God to grow every tree that is pleasant to the sight, and good for food; the tree of life also in the midst of the garden, and THE TREE OF KNOWLEDGE OF GOOD AND EVIL.

Genesis 2:9

Paul, the apostle, is one of the great examples of a minister who managed to follow the Lord. He was fresh till the end and the anointing never diminished. Right up till the end of his ministry he lived under the guidance of the Lord.

When you are following the Lord, it may seem as though you are erratic; not following a particular pattern.

I can understand this, because following God is not the same as following a rigid formula. God is not a formula; God is not a computer program!

Paul received different instructions from the Lord. At one time, he said he had been instructed by God to be full and to abound. In other words, he was to enjoy prosperity and blessings. In the same breath, he said he had been instructed by the Lord to abase and to endure hunger.

I know both how to be abased, and I know how to abound: every where and in all things I AM INSTRUCTED BOTH to be full and to be hungry, both to abound and to suffer need.

Philippians 4:12

Both instructions came from God. It is not a good thing to be in need. The tree of good and evil will always guide you away from things that will bring you into need. But this was God's will and direction to Paul. At other times, he had the exact opposite direction from the Lord.

Twenty-one Days' Fasting

I would have missed some of the greatest events of my ministry if I had rigidly followed traditions that I had developed. Twenty-one days of fasting is a tradition of our church. I could never see myself going through a year without that annual fast.

I did this for years without fail and then one day, I received my first-ever invitation to South America to minister at exactly the same time we held the twenty-one days' fast.

I decided not to go on this trip because my protection and sustenance now lay in this twenty-one days' fast at the beginning of the year (and not in God). I had more faith in the twenty-one days' fast than in God.

After years of serving the Lord, I knew that the way to success and achievement lay in the formula of twenty-one days' fasting at the beginning of the year. I knew the formula that would keep me alive and I intended to stick to it.

To cut a long story short, I ended up breaking my good tradition and going to South America instead of fasting for twenty-one days with the church. On that trip, all the doors to South American countries flung open. I suddenly had a ministry in the Spanish-speaking world of Latin America, which God had prepared for me.

Like Paul, I was receiving an instruction to do something quite contrary to what I had done previously. Paul had been told to be full and on another occasion he had been commanded to be hungry. Only by following these apparently contrary instructions, could he stay in the company of the Lord. You see, this is the point at which we part company with the Lord.

By not fasting for twenty-one days and obeying the Lord, I entered into another phase of my ministry and found myself in countries like, Argentina, Bolivia, Mexico, Paraguay, Colombia and so on.

From my background of living and working in Korle Gonno, Accra, I see no link which could bring me into these places. On that same fateful trip, I saw every miracle I had ever dreamed of seeing. I even saw the first person raised from the dead in my ministry. It is the Lord who opened the door and I almost missed it because of the tree of the knowledge of good and evil. I knew what was good and what was right and I was not prepared to listen to God anymore. I had my own tree.

Paul, Please Go to Prison

And when he was come unto us, he took Paul's girdle, and bound his own hands and feet, and said, THUS SAITH THE HOLY GHOST, SO SHALL THE JEWS AT JERUSALEM BIND THE MAN that owneth this girdle, and shall deliver him into the hands of the Gentiles.

And when we heard these things, both we, and they of that place, besought him not to go up to Jerusalem.

Then Paul answered, What mean ye to weep and to break mine heart? for I AM READY NOT TO BE BOUND ONLY, BUT ALSO TO DIE at Jerusalem for the name of the Lord Jesus.

Acts 21:11-13

Most ministers today would consider going to prison as a kind of curse. In our society, it would be the lowest place to fall to. In fact, it would be almost impossible to direct any of us to prison. We would do anything to avoid prison.

But not so with Paul. He declared, "I am ready to go to prison in Jerusalem." He knew that when he got to Jerusalem, he would not be staying at the Sheraton Hotel but he would be in prison. Even though prison is an evil thing, he went towards it and embraced it because that is what God wanted.

God may want you to do something that hitherto you have labelled evil, bad or wrong!

It would interest you to know that Paul wrote most of his letters while in prison. Two thousand years after the death of Paul, the churches he planted no longer exist. However, the letters he wrote from prison are being used over and over again. It is quite clear that it was when he was finally in prison that he began to bear eternal fruit.

Going around preaching and planting churches is a good thing. We would choose it above going to prison. But God wanted Paul to stop planting churches and to go to prison to testify of Jesus from there.

Brothers, the wisdom of God cannot be compared to the tree of the knowledge of good and evil. All knowledge is found in God but not all knowledge is found in the tree of the knowledge of good and evil. "In whom are hid all the treasures of wisdom and knowledge" (Colossians 2:3).

Peter Argues with God

The Apostle Peter had grown up knowing that certain things were right and certain things were wrong. Being a devout Jew, Peter would never eat certain animals. And Peter would also not have anything to do with Gentiles according to his Jewish tradition.

But God wanted to take the Gospel beyond the Jews. He needed a vessel who would obey Him and set aside all the knowledge of good and evil that he had.

Peter had a dream:

On the morrow, as they went on their journey, and drew nigh unto the city, Peter went up upon the housetop to pray about the sixth hour:

And he became very hungry, and would have eaten: but while they made ready, he fell into a trance,

And saw heaven opened, and a certain vessel descending unto him, as it had been a great sheet knit at the four corners, and let down to the earth:

Wherein were all manner of fourfooted beasts of the earth, and wild beasts, and creeping things, and fowls of the air.

And there came a voice to him, Rise, Peter; kill, and eat.

But Peter said, Not so, Lord; for I have never eaten any thing that is common or unclean.

And the voice spake unto him again the second time, What God hath cleansed, that call not thou common.

This was done thrice: and the vessel was received up again into heaven.

Acts 10:9-16

Peter was now arguing with the Lord because he knew what was right and he knew what was wrong. God could not tell him to do things that were wrong.

Oh, how easy it is to become rigid and crystallized in one direction when we have served God for a while. If it were not for the grace of God and His mercies, we would all be lost in delusions of self-righteousness.

CHAPTER 5

Christ and the Tree

And out of the ground made the LORD God to grow every tree that is pleasant to the sight, and good for food; the tree of life also in the midst of the garden, and THE TREE OF KNOWLEDGE OF GOOD AND EVIL.

Genesis 2:9

As you go higher with the Lord, the battle will be between the good side of the tree of the knowledge of good and evil and God's will for your life.

The ultimate will of God is discovered in the words of Jesus. There are no purer words and greater words than the words of Jesus. There are many things that Jesus said that go against the traditional knowledge of good and evil.

Please do not use this book as an excuse to do bad things. This book is bringing you closer to God. This book is giving you a deeper revelation of the purposes of God for your life.

Is Hatred a Good Thing or a Bad Thing?

If any man come to me, and hate not his father, and mother, and wife, and children, and brethren, and sisters, yea, and his own life also, he cannot be my disciple.

Luke 14:26

In this Scripture, Jesus is clearly saying that there is a time when hatred for father, mother, wife and children will be a necessary qualification to be His disciple.

We all know that Jesus is love. God is love and He loves us greatly. Greater love has no man than the love of Jesus. And yet, we find Jesus saying that there will be a time and a place for hatred.

Hate Your Father and Mother?

God's Word teaches us to honour our fathers and our mothers. How can Jesus now speak of hatred for fathers and mothers? To hate your father and your mother is a very difficult and hard saying! Perhaps it is too deep for most of us. Perhaps most of you do not understand what this means.

I do not blame you. It is a hard and difficult saying but they are still the words of Jesus. There is a place and a time where or

25

when you must hate your own father and own mother in order to please God.

Hate Your Wife?

The Word teaches us to love our wives; yet, here we find Jesus telling us that you may have to hate your wife in order to be His disciple.

This is another equally hard saying. Many people have come to a point where this Scripture must be obeyed but they could not understand that they were at a point when they must obey this verse. This Scripture does not register on the mind of the average believer and is difficult to understand. Perhaps, you are not to understand it but to obey it if and when such a day dawns on your life.

Hate Your Children?

Hate your children? Are we reading aright? Did Jesus say you would have to hate your children in order to be His disciple?

Traditionally, children are cared for, nurtured, cherished and loved. And here comes Jesus proclaiming a time when hatred for your own children would be necessary for ministry. Wow!

Jesus, who said, "...Suffer the little children to come unto me..." now says you will have to hate your children.

Anyone who has eaten too much of the tree of the knowledge of good and evil cannot receive these instructions. You will know too much about caring for children for your mind to comprehend something like this. Jesus ends by saying, you must hate even your own life!

Hate Your Life?

The instruction to hate your own life is contrary to an earlier instruction that Jesus gave when He said you must love your neighbour as you love yourself. So in one breath, Jesus says we should love ourselves and in another He says we should hate our own selves.

If you want to stay with your tree of information of good and evil, you are likely to lose contact with God at a point.

Christianity is not based on reasonable logic. It is based on God's will being carried out by God's Son, Jesus Christ.

It is not logical to send your son to a brutal death at the hands of wicked murderers. It is irrational and illogical for anyone to do something like that. It is not a good thing. In fact, by our standards, it is a bad thing to send someone somewhere, when we know very well that he will perish there.

If God had followed that protocol, none of us would be saved. I believe with all my heart that the ministry will fail to save mankind if the bearers of the Gospel become traditional and steeped in old ways, unable to change, unable to bend and unable to flow with the Lord.

Why We Prefer the Tree

There are a number of reasons why we prefer the tree of the knowledge of good and evil to the true will of God.

1.   Following the will of God involves humility.

Many times, we will have to swallow our own words in order to do the true will of God. Many times, we would have to admit that we've been wrong about something in order to follow the will of God.

There are times it is very humiliating to make a U-turn and embrace what you have insulted and ridiculed for years.

As usual, pride is the stumbling block to receiving the gift of God.

Many people have ridiculed churches or pastors, which they now belong to or listen to regularly. It took humility to accept what God was doing.

2.   Following the tree of the knowledge of good and evil gives a sense of independence from God.

The prideful and evil nature of man loves to be independent from God. We want to take decisions on our own and to be free from the need to have to consult anyone.

King David, however, loved to inquire of the Lord and to consult with Him constantly. That is why he was a man after God's own heart. God loved David because David kept going to Him.

Wouldn't you love to work with someone who keeps coming to you and never develops an air of independence and pride?

How painful it is to meet these prideful and independent individuals whom you trained and raised up but who try hard to erase any remembrance of your input in their lives.

It is time to follow God into every new season and any new wave of the Spirit. Dear friend, you can regain the crispness and newness of spirit that you once had.

You can rise into higher things that God has called you for. God wants to raise you up with a brightness that will never fade.

It is the tree of the knowledge of good and evil that has led to the overwhelming desolation of our world. It is that tree of knowledge which has made much of the church so withered and so pale.

Knowledge cannot and will never be a substitute for the Lord God Jehovah. All the glory belongs to God and unless we stay close to Him forever, the shine will go away!